DATE DUE			

ALLIGATORS
AND
CROCODILES

CONTENTS

© Aladdin Books Ltd 1990

*First published in
the United States in 1990 by*
Gloucester Press
387 Park Avenue South
New York NY 10016

Design Rob Hillier, Andy Wilkinson
Editor Fiona Robertson
Photo Research Cecilia Weston-Baker
Illustrations Ron Hayward Associates

All rights reserved

Printed in Belgium

Library of Congress Cataloging-in-Publication Data

Bright, Michael.
    Alligators and crocodiles / Michael Bright.
      p.cm.--(Project wildlife)
    Summary: Describes efforts to save the dwindling alligator and
crocodile populations from extinction. Includes facts on the
appearance and daily activities of various species.
    ISBN 0-531-17245-7
    1. Alligators--Juvenile literature. 2. Crocodiles--Juvenile
literature. 3. Wildlife conservation--Juvenile literature.
    I. Title. II. Series.
    [DNLM: 1. Alligators. 2. Crocodiles. 3. Wildlife conservation.]
QL666.C925B75   1990
597.98--dc20

90-3225   CIP   AC

ALLIGATORS AND CROCODILES

Michael Bright

Franklin Watts
London : New York : Toronto : Sydney

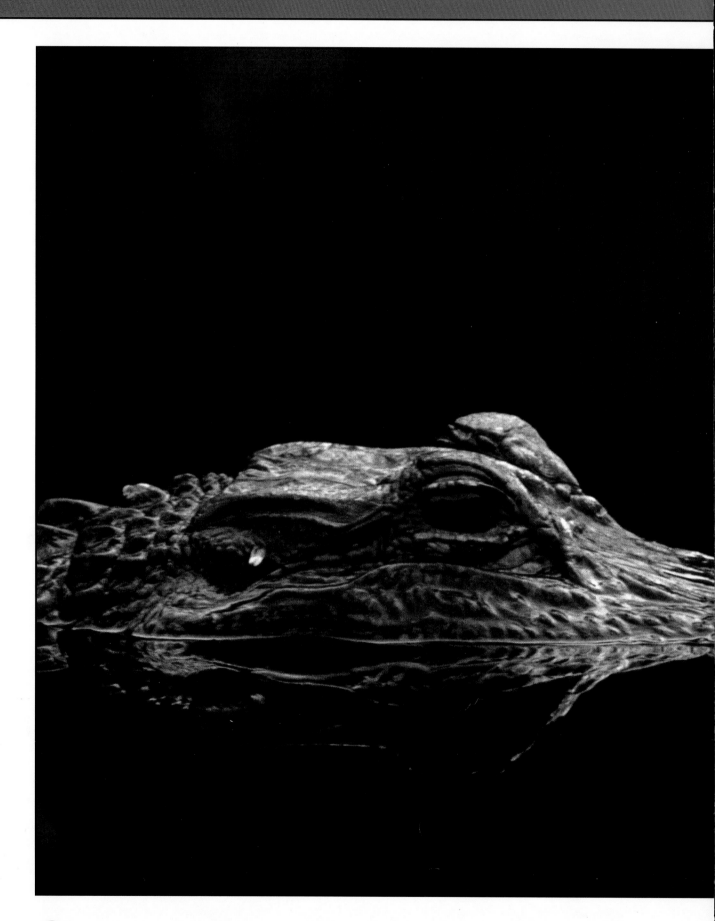

A Mississippi alligator lies
motionless but alert.

Introduction

Alligators and crocodiles have an image problem. Most people think of them as ugly and not at all "cuddly." In some countries they are treated as pests because the larger ones occasionally eat people. However, conservationists are worried by the threat of extinction which faces many species, due to the value placed on their skins and the disappearance of their living space. And it is difficult to have much sympathy for these unattractive and potentially dangerous creatures. Few people would care if they were simply wiped out.

Alligators and crocodiles have survived since the time of the dinosaurs, 225-65 million years ago. But what nature created and developed over millions of years, man looks set to destroy in just a few decades.

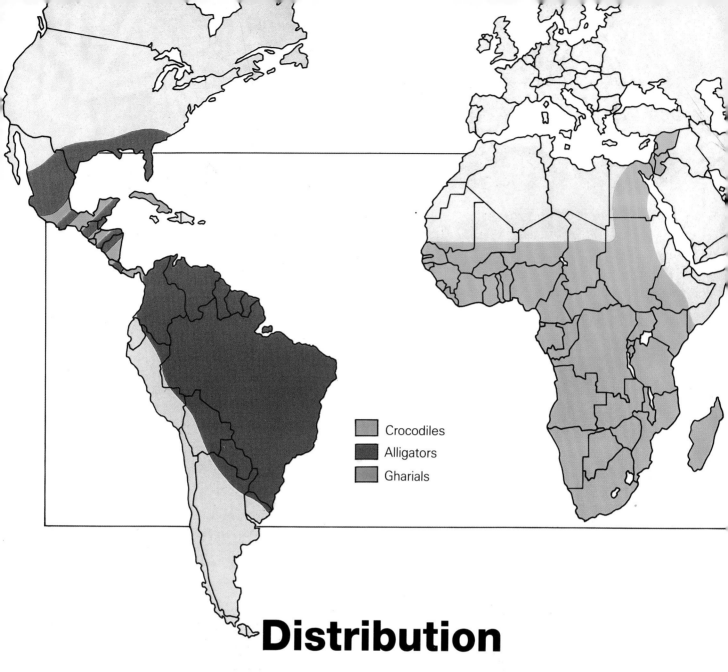

Crocodiles
Alligators
Gharials

Distribution

Although the present distribution of crocodilians may give an impression that some species are doing well, the truth is that the populations, though widely spread, are very thin on the ground. The southern tip of Africa has few wild Nile crocs. Populations of gharials in Pakistan, and Chinese alligators in the Far East are very patchy. But it is not all gloom; Johnstoni's crocodiles are spreading into Western Australia, and there are crocs in Sri Lanka.

Alligators, crocodiles, caimans and gharials have been killed indiscriminately throughout the world. Long ago, across the southern part of the United States, for example, the majority of rivers contained American alligators. Then the European settlers came, and by the mid-20th century, most alligators had been killed.

The great Nile River once teemed with Nile crocodiles. By 1800 they had disappeared from the delta, and by 1900 were absent below Aswan. Until the 1940s, all the rivers of Belize had Morelet's crocodile. By 1960, very few were left anywhere. Such widespread exploitation has led to a sharp decline in population numbers.

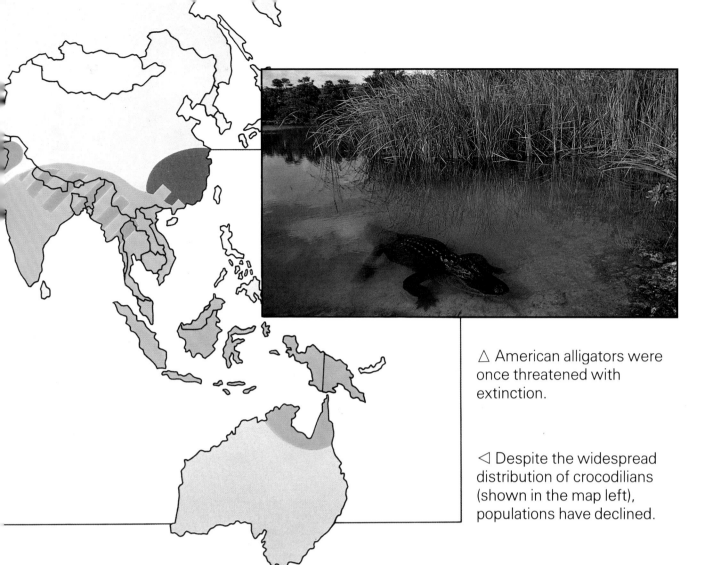

△ American alligators were once threatened with extinction.

◁ Despite the widespread distribution of crocodilians (shown in the map left), populations have declined.

In Papua New Guinea, saltwater crocodiles were exterminated in parts of the Fly and Sepik Rivers. In a 1973 survey of Indian rivers which were once teeming with gharials, only six were found. In the same year, a survey of the Orinoco in Colombia revealed just 300 surviving crocodiles. The Chinese alligator in the Yangtze River was once greatly feared by local people, but is now rarely seen. And the Siamese crocodile is almost unknown in the wild today.

There are four main types of crocodilians. The blunt-snouted alligator mostly lives in rivers, such as the Mississippi, and wetlands, such as the Everglades, in southeastern parts of North America. The exception is the Chinese alligator in the Yangtze River. The more rounded-nosed caimans are found in the tropical parts of Central and South America, such as the Amazon basin. The long-nosed gharial is confined to the rivers of northern India, Nepal, Pakistan and Bangladesh.

The variably-snouted crocodiles are widely distributed across Africa, southern Asia and Australasia. There is also a species in the Orinoco River of Venezuela. The Cuban crocodile is confined to two swamps in Cuba, and the American crocodile is found in Florida, Central America, northern South America and certain Caribbean islands.

Killing crocs

Crocodiles have always been killed by local people for food, clothing and adornments such as jewelry. They never took too many. Using nets, traps, spears, harpoons and baited lines they caught only the number they needed. But when commercial hunters moved in with modern weapons and slaughtered crocodile populations, mostly for their valuable skins, the local people were deprived of a valuable resource.

Some native traps were ingenious. In Guyana, a four-pronged device, spring-loaded with twigs and tied with agouti gut, was eaten by the croc. Digestive juices caused the trap to spring in the croc's stomach, killing it.

◁ The old picture shows people killing crocodiles. They were so afraid of them that some felt the only good crocodile was a dead one. This fear was evident in Africa when people on river steamers used to shoot at crocodiles on river banks, killing them not for food, but for bravado.

▽ Alligators are best hunted at night. When a flashlight is directed at an animal, the light is reflected from a silvery layer at the back of the eyes. A hunter simply shoots between the two reflections and hits the beast square in the middle of its head. Or, he can loop a noose around the head and hoist it out.

By the 1960s, the numbers of alligators and crocodiles throughout the world were considerably reduced. The decline was due, in part, to the introduction of modern transportation and weapons. Guns replaced spears. Helicopters and trucks replaced canoes. In some parts of South America helicopter gunships equipped with high-powered searchlights, and armed with machine guns, went to hunt crocodiles and caimans at night. In the morning men in boats collected the carcasses.

The increase in trade has affected local hunters in two ways: first, their crocodiles have been slaughtered, and second, the smaller fish, on which they depend for food, are eaten by the larger fish whose numbers were previously controlled by the crocodiles. By removing the top predators – the crocodiles and caimans – hunters have upset the natural balance between predators and prey.

The trade

Over two million crocodilian skins are traded each year. Of these, the majority (1-1.5 million) are from the spectacled caiman, a species which has disappeared from the Atlantic coast areas of South America and which is now being pursued and eradicated along rivers further inland. Some are being farmed for their skins in Taiwan. The other 500,000 skins are from other crocodile species, including a legal trade of 31,000 alligator skins valued at $4.6 million in the United States. The rest of the skins are taken and traded illegally by poachers and smugglers.

Only the skin from the belly and flanks is used commercially. The rest is too knobby. The giant saltwater crocodile of southern Asia and northern Australia has the largest and smoothest skin. In the 1970s population numbers in the world were reduced by 100,000 animals a year.

Crocodile skins are made into luxury goods – shoes, suitcases, handbags, watch bands, fancy belts and the bindings of personal organizers.

▷ This macabre keyring is made from the dried head of a baby crocodilian. Thousands of youngsters are killed to make these obscene trinkets. The killing is made all the more senseless by the fact that these baby crocodiles must survive to grow up into the next generation. If the babies are killed, there will be no adults to breed in the future and the species will eventually die out altogether.

▽ It is difficult to see the attraction of a stuffed baby crocodile dressed in a golfing outfit, like those in the photograph below. People in Florida buy live baby caimans as pets. When they get too large to keep they are most probably killed.

In 1986, Italy surpassed France and joined Japan as one of the main recipients of crocodile skins. The United States provides one of the major retail markets. In a survey of leading American stores, TRAFFIC USA – a body that monitors wildlife trade in the United States – found that crocodile skin products included handbags costing $880 and belts at $235. The profits are enormous, although the countries where the animals are killed do not receive as much as those that manufacture and retail the goods.

In Belize, a Morelet's crocodile, which has one of the finest hides, is bought by a local dealer from the hunter for $5 a foot (30cm); a licensed European dealer buys them for $7 a foot; the Belgian holding company purchases them for $10-15 and sells them to the Italian manufacturer. Of the $2,500 that a single hide will yield, only 2 percent will get back to Belize. The retailer takes the largest percentage in this illegal operation.

▽ Various parts of crocodiles are used in traditional medicines in the Far East. It is said that the gall bladder helps women in childbirth. It is also good for healing wounds, and dispersing boils, and can be used as a remedy for a bite from a rabid dog.

Poaching and smuggling

In 1988, another smuggling operation was uncovered in which 2,000 baby crocodiles were shipped live from Colombia to Taiwan by way of Panama and Madrid. Only 500 survived the journey.

The profits in the crocodile skin trade are so large, poachers go to great lengths to continue their illegal trade. In 1988, TRAFFIC Japan uncovered a multinational smuggling operation which shipped 120,000 caiman skins from South America to Japan.

The investigators followed a trail of forged or stolen documents involving officials from many countries. It is thought the animals were killed illegally in Brazil in 1987 and smuggled to Paraguay. They were shipped to Yokohama from Uruguay, but were turned away from Japan because they had the incorrect papers. The skins were then moved to Thailand via South Korea, Taiwan, and Singapore. In Singapore documents were issued giving Colombia as the country of origin for one batch, although Colombia has not legally shipped skins to Japan since 1972.

In Thailand the skins received bogus papers. By Japanese law, shipments from countries that have not signed the Convention on Trade in Endangered Species (CITES) can be questioned and rejected, but those from CITES countries must be allowed in. Thailand is a signatory of CITES. The bogus permits allowed the smugglers to get around Japanese customs laws.

It would be very difficult for a nonspecialist to tell if it is legal or illegal to trade in the crocodile skin on the left. This provides a loophole which smugglers can exploit. Documents with the name of a common species in which it is legal to trade can easily deceive officials.

The jacare caiman is shipped illegally in this way. It is protected in Brazil, yet skins reach the United States each year. At US customs, officials may be unable to distinguish the hides of this rare species from those of more common species, and they are allowed to enter.

These hunters will get very little money for the skins that they have poached. Yet many will take the risk and kill alligators, caimans and crocodiles illegally. In Brazil, the fine for poaching is no more than a speeding ticket.

In Sarawak, there are reports of an illegal trade in live crocodiles. About 200 young crocodiles are caught and smuggled to farms in Singapore each year. Here they are reared, and their skins used for illegal trading and commercial purposes.

Habitat destruction

All over the world, alligators and crocodiles have come into conflict with human activities. They are losing living space, are harassed, and are being poisoned. The American alligator suffered badly from habitat loss in the 1970s. The desire of many Americans for a dream home in the sun resulted in a property boom in Florida and Louisiana. In Florida alone, the development of six counties resulted in the disappearance of 23 percent of the alligator's habitat. Only a ban on hunting ensured that alligator populations in the southeastern United States were maintained.

People disturb crocodiles just as much as they seem to upset people. Along African rivers, tourist boats are disturbing female Nile crocodiles that are guarding their nests. The mothers are frightened away, and nest predators then sneak in and eat the eggs.

△ Brown caiman, which feed on crabs, once inhabited the mangroves that grew at the mouth of Colombia's Magdalena River.

But the mangroves have been destroyed, even in officially protected areas, such as the Isla de Samanaca National Park.

Upstream, the killing of manatees has created a haven for the few surviving caimans. Waterweed has provided somewhere to hide.

Life in rivers is often seriously affected by the pollution from industry and agriculture. In mining areas, waste discharged into the rivers kills the fish on which crocodiles feed and can poison the crocs themselves. In Papua New Guinea (PNG), gold mine wastes have wiped out the few surviving saltwater crocodiles. In northeastern Brazil, the Grand Carajas project plans to bring open cast mines and aluminum smelters to the cleared forest. River pollution from this new industry could mean the end of the few caimans that have survived the poachers.

▽ Logging (below) and farming affects all life in forest areas, both in the trees and in the rivers. South America's tiny smooth-fronted caiman has a heavily armored hide that is unsuitable for making leather. It is safe from poachers. But its numbers are dwindling because its tropical forest habitat is being invaded by loggers and cattle ranchers. It could become extinct.

Problem crocs

Chinese alligators have always been feared and disliked. Chinese peasants used to kill them on sight and children were encouraged to destroy their eggs – simply because they were regarded as an inconvenient nuisance. Alligators were unpopular with both fish-farmers and duck-breeders, and people were so afraid of them that they were eliminated from the places where building and farming developments took place. The indiscriminate use of pesticides and fertilizers in the fields bordering their home river, the Yangtze, poisoned their food and almost wiped out the few that survived in remote areas.

The American alligator, however, is a nuisance because its recovery has been so successful. In Florida, where the property boom has been matched by an alligator baby boom, almost every ditch and pool seems to have its resident alligators. Officers of the Florida Game and Freshwater Fish Commission are summoned regularly to water sports lakes, ponds on golf courses, and swimming pools to remove vagrant alligators. Fourteen official alligator trappers respond to nearly seven thousand complaints a year. At one time they relocated the misdemeanants deeper into the Everglade swamps, but today the loss of wetlands coupled with the increase in alligators, has meant that the animals are killed and their skins sold to the skin trade. And the authorities cannot take any chances. Nearly one hundred people have been attacked in the past ten years.

Theron McBride is a diver who recovers golf balls from pools on golf courses. Imagine his surprise when he was seized by a 2.5m long alligator. McBride survived the attack, the alligator did not.

▷ An alligator crossing a road is not an unusual sight in southern Florida, but it still causes some consternation among the residents.

In some places they have been known to attack. One British holidaymaker was attacked while water skiing, and was lucky to escape.

Crocodile farms

The only hope for the survival of some species of crocodiles and alligators is the crocodile farm. The Siamese crocodile, for example, has been reduced to about 40 individuals in the wild in Thailand and only survives in large numbers in a farm at Samut Prakan. During the 1960s in Papua New Guinea, a thriving crocodile skin industry was threatened with closure when most of the saltwater crocodiles were killed.

After 20 years of hunting, it was decided to rear crocs in farms. The first skins were marketed in 1979 and accounted for only 2 percent of the exports. In 1989, the proportion had risen to 40 percent. Today, the farms are so successful that there are plans to release crocodiles back into the wild. Similar farms have been set up in various parts of the world to breed different species of crocodiles, as well as Chinese alligators.

▷ Disease can be a problem in crocodile farms due to overcrowding. Farms in PNG are sited next to poultry breeding farms for a ready supply of food. Most obtain their eggs from the wild. In Singapore many stores and small farms rear crocodiles as a sideline to their main business, but the animals are kept in poor conditions.

▽ The gharial was on the brink of extinction and so eggs were collected in boxes (below). When the captive youngsters can defend themselves against predators, they are released.

Protective measures

Seventeen species of alligators, crocodiles, caimans and gharials are considered so rare that they cannot be traded internationally, except in countries where populations are thriving. They are on Appendix I, the highest level of protection afforded by the Convention on International Trade in Endangered Species (CITES).

Unfortunately, controls on trade in reptile hides are weak, and it is easy to cheat the system. So officials from the main importing nations – Italy, Japan, Singapore, the United States, France, Switzerland, and West Germany – must be extra vigilant in their attempts to reduce the illicit trade. The European countries get most of their skins from crocodile farms in Africa and New Guinea. Japan, however, imports skins from South America, where poaching and smuggling are rife.

The species which are fully protected include: Chinese alligator; jacare and black caiman; Cuban, American, Orinoco, Philippine, Siamese, Morelet's and African broad-nosed and dwarf crocodiles; and Indian and false gharials.

▽ Faced with the extinction of the gharial (seen in captivity below) in 1973, the Indian government created several reserves into which the young bred in captivity could be released.

The American alligator was close to extinction in the 1960s and it was officially protected in most of the southern states. As soon as hunting was stopped and restrictions were placed on habitat destruction, populations rapidly recovered. Even limited hunting in the 1970s had little effect on the recovery, and the alligator was taken off the endangered list.

By 1980, the export of hides was legally permitted. Between 10,000 and 16,000 are allowed to be culled each year. The trade is strictly regulated. Meat and hides must be labeled. Heads and feet are sold as curios. Gall bladders are sold to the Far East for traditional medicines. The American alligator was not only brought back from the brink of extinction, but it also helped to finance its own survival.

▽ Tourists can watch wild American alligators in the Florida Everglades from boardwalks like the one below. They can also see them in alligator farms which have been operating in the United States since the late 19th century. The animals are mostly tourist attractions, although some are killed for their hides. However, the contribution to the trade is small — only about a tenth of those killed in the wild. About 1,000 hides a year are supplied from about 30 farms in Louisiana, Florida, and one farm in Texas.

Research

In order to conserve alligators and crocodiles it is critical to understand the way in which they live, and how their bodies work. Some specimens are caught and measured and then released. They can be recognized in the future by cutting away some of the scutes, or scales, on the tail. Measurements taken on future occasions will give researchers an idea of how fast each one grows. This helps to establish when individuals reach maturity and become ready to breed.

One important discovery was that crocodiles breed late in life – about eight to ten years old in the large American alligator and the saltwater crocodile. This information would be crucial for any management plan. If, say, all the older members of a population were culled, there would be none ready to take their place. The rate of increase of that population would slow rapidly, and could disappear altogether.

In some parts of the world people kill crocodiles because they are afraid of being attacked by them. But research in eastern India has shown that crocodile attacks are less frequent than was originally thought. In a ten year study in the Bhitarkanika crocodile sanctuary, only four attacks have been recorded, despite large numbers of visitors.

▽ These gharials have been given radio collars. Each collar emits a signal that can be identified and followed. In this way the daily activities of gharials can be monitored, and they can be better studied and understood.

▽ These researchers are taking an American alligator's temperature. They have discovered that alligators are sensitive to excessive changes in temperature. A rise of only 13.5°F above the usual can be fatal. Therefore the alligator digs a small pond or "gator" hole in which it can keep cool during the day in the dry season.

Research into the life of the American alligator has revealed how important its existence is to the entire animal and plant community. It eats large fish, which enables smaller fish to grow. "Gator" holes provide a refuge for other aquatic life during droughts, and nest mounds form small islands on which trees can grow. Herons and egrets nest in these trees, safe from prowling raccoons because the female alligator is on guard below. Hunting upsets this natural balance.

▽ Nest temperatures are also measured. Researchers can determine if the offspring will be males or females depending on the temperature. Below 86°F produces females, above 89°F produces males. This is important in captive breeding.

The future

The majority of alligators and crocodiles have a bleak future. Crocodile farms do not contribute greatly to the trade, so most species are still killed in the wild. There is greater profit to be made if crocodiles are hunted legally or illegally rather than reared in captivity. An American alligator, for example, costs $110 to raise and sells for $300. Also, the market is unstable. In the 1980s prices tumbled. Processed hides from Thailand slumped from $250 to $90 each. Farms have had to keep animals alive until prices recover.

▽ The Nile crocodile below still has its skin. Its relatives are not so lucky. Chad and Gabon export 35,000 Nile crocodile skins each year, mostly taken from the wild. South Africa and Zimbabwe contribute a couple of thousand hides a year from crocodile farms. From 1950 to 1980, over three million. Nile crocodiles were killed for their valuable skins.

Some species, like the American alligator, have recovered from the time of widespread killing in the 1960s. Others, like the black caiman, have populations that are just one hundredth of their former size. Logging, farming and industrial development have taken precedence over wildlife conservation. Only a few are bred in captivity. However, there is some hope in the growing trend to conserve the remaining populations of many species. The slaughter has not stopped, but it has slowed down. Successful captive breeding could slow it down even more. But the continued demand for skins means that many more wild alligators and crocodiles must die.

Top predators, such as the alligator and the crocodile, are slow to breed. They take many years to reach maturity and face all the normal hazards of life, such as predation when young. Consequently, when the large, mature specimens are killed it takes a long time for others to replace them in the breeding cycle and keep the population healthy.

△ This egg was laid in the wild. But the hatchling will spend its life in a farm.

Crocodilian fact file 1

The largest living reptile is the saltwater crocodile. It can reach 9m (30ft) in length, but today is most unlikely to exceed 6.0m (20ft) and weigh 1300kg (1 ton). Gharials have been found to grow to similar lengths. Nile crocodiles and American alligators reach 6m (20ft). American, Orinoco and mugger crocodiles can grow to 5m (16ft). The largest known crocodile was a fossil gharial found in the hills of the Siwalik Range on the northern India-Nepal border. It was estimated to be 18m (59ft) in length.

Size and Difference

The shape of the head and snout of crocodiles, caiman, gharials and alligators is dependent on the kind of food that they catch and eat. Gharials and long-snouted crocodiles have an elongated, slender snout for catching fish. It moves easily through the water and can swipe to the side to grab a fish. Muggers and alligators have short, blunt snouts with powerful jaws that can crack open turtle shells and grab mammals and birds that come to the water to drink. Nile and saltwater crocodiles have rounded snouts and are generalized feeders; they eat whatever is available including fish, birds and the dead carcasses of animals that have drowned in the river.

Crocodiles have short limbs, but when "high walking" they can lift the body from the ground. This is a relatively slow method of moving, but muggers have been known to travel vast distances from dried up ponds to seek a new home. Australian freshwater crocodiles have been seen to "gallop." When the crocodile wants to move in a hurry it "toboggans" over the mud. The front feet have five digits and no webbing, whereas the rear pair have four and the toes are webbed. In the water the crocodile floats "tail heavy," but as it moves the body becomes horizontal. Propulsion in the water is by lashing the very powerful, laterally compressed tail. When swimming the legs are held by the crocodile's side.

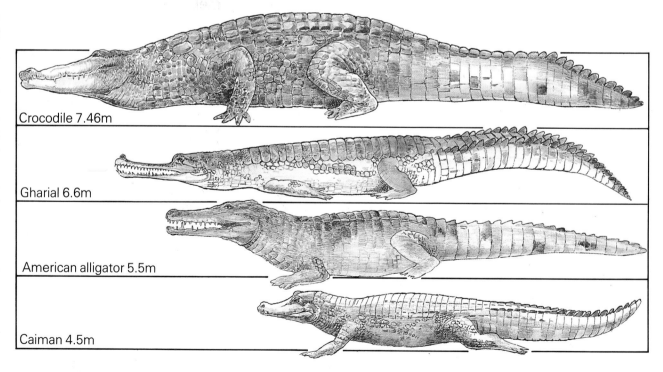

Crocodile 7.46m

Gharial 6.6m

American alligator 5.5m

Caiman 4.5m

Distinctive Features

Although its appearance seems primitive the crocodile in fact has advanced features. The heart ventricles are completely divided and so more oxygenated blood is pumped to the brain. The "thinking" part of the brain is more developed than in other reptiles. This enables the crocodile to learn things, rather than to behave instinctively.

Crocodiles are well adapted for an aquatic life. A third eyelid, or nictitating membrane, sweeps sideways across the eye to give more protection when submerged. The ears and nostrils can close. And a false glottis, or throat valve, at the back of the mouth enables a crocodile to swallow when under the water. Alligators can stay underwater for over five hours.

Crocodiles can see and hear very well out of water. Their ears are highly sensitive. They are alert to the slightest movement or noise. American alligators have been known to be able to find their way home. It seems that they can detect the earth's magnetic field. From this information they are then able to figure out where they are at that moment, and in which direction they should head to return to their own river or lake. It is thought that they might also take celestial bearings from the sun, stars and the moon. In an experiment in the United States, a scientist released 285 young alligators at a point some way from their home site. All but one headed off in the right direction and found their way home.

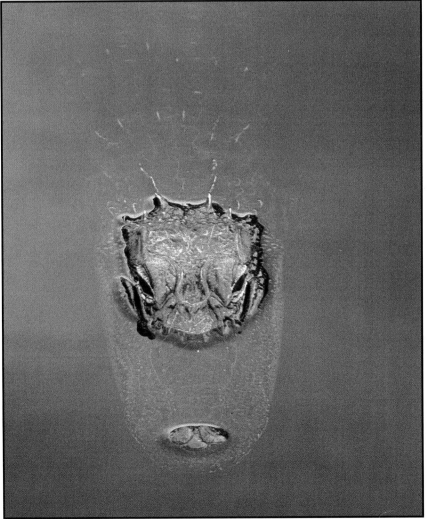

The eyes and nostrils of the American alligator (left) and all other crocodilians are set high on the head. The animal can lie just below the surface like a plank, yet still see and breathe. In bright sunlight the eyes are reduced to vertical slits, but in faint light, such as at dawn and dusk, they see well. This enables them to hunt.

Crocodilian fact file 2

Habitat

Most crocodiles, caimans, alligators and gharials are found in freshwater areas, and sometimes in saltwater in mangrove swamps. Saltwater crocodiles prefer estuaries, but have been seen far out to sea. One was seen 30 miles to the north of New Zealand and another landed in the Cocos Keeling Islands, 601 miles from the nearest land. Nile crocodiles may be found in groups of twenty or so individuals. A large male will dominate the group. He asserts his position by slapping his head on the water. He is the first to leave the water each day to bask on the bank.

Basking

Most of a crocodile's day is spent basking in the sun. But if the body temperature is raised above 100°F the animal could die.

To gain heat in the morning, or lose it rapidly at midday, it opens its mouth (like the alligator below). In the mouth the blood vessels are close to the skin.

Rivers warm up slowly in the morning, so a crocodile heats up by basking. At night the water cools slowly, so it spends the night submerged to keep warm.

Teeth

The shape of crocodile teeth is related to the prey caught. Gharials (below) have sharp piercing teeth to hold on to wriggling fish. Nile crocodiles have teeth that tear and can hold on to large prey. A tooth can fall out during a struggle, but in the pulp cavity is a replacement tooth.

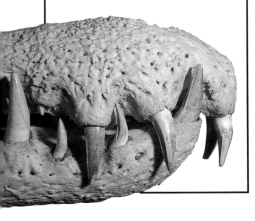

Food and feeding

Many crocodiles rely on surprise to obtain a meal. Hidden below the water, with only eyes and nostrils showing, a crocodile will drift slowly toward the victim and then make a rapid dash. The Nile crocodile will wait at the water's edge for animals to come down to drink. Although it will eat anything from zebras to domestic livestock and man, 70 percent of a Nile crocodile's food is fish, including catfish, eels and sharks. A large carcass is often dragged away to a spot safe from other crocodiles and eaten at leisure. Pieces are torn off in a characteristic way. The crocodile grabs a piece of flesh, and then rotates it violently in order to twist it off.

Humans are on the menu of several species of crocodile. In fact, saltwater and Nile crocodiles are thought to account for more fatalities each year than sharks. American alligators (like the one above with a blue heron) have a penchant for water birds. Young crocodiles and alligators often eat different food from their parents. They tackle large insects and small crabs, frogs, lizards and fish. Crocodiles occasionally succumb to predation by other creatures. A life-and-death struggle was once witnessed between a 6ft long Nile crocodile and a 15ft long African python. The python coiled itself around the crocodile, and after a two-hour battle, squeezed it to death.

Crocodilian fact file 3

Courtship

It is difficult to tell a male crocodile from a female except in one species. The male gharial has a bulbous, potlike structure on the end of its snout. Male crocodiles tend to be larger than females. In courtship a male Nile crocodile will try to impress females by submerging and bubbling water from his nostrils and mouth. An interested female arches her back and then raises her head with her mouth open. The male responds by rasping his lower jaw across her back. He swims alongside, and places his front and hind limbs over her body. During copulation they sink to the bottom. After about two months the female is ready to lay her eggs.

Nesting/Eggs

The female seeks out a nest site that is unlikely to flood. Gharials and Nile crocodiles dig a flask-shaped hole in the ground and then carefully cover it with soil. Saltwater crocodiles and American alligators build mounds of vegetation that can be 10 feet in diameter and three feet high. The temperature at the center of the rotting leaves and stems is a constant 86-89.5°F. Most species mount a watchful guard on the nest against nest predators such as monitor lizards. Nile crocodiles may have sites where several females nest close together. Anything approaching is greeted with growls and an open-mouthed threat display.

The eggs are laid and guided gently into tiers within the nest hollow by the hind feet. Incubation for Nile and saltwater crocodiles is about 90 days, and 60-70 days for American alligators. Black caimans and gharials vary from 60-90 days depending on the weather and temperature, and Chinese alligators take 70 days.

Crocodile eggs have hard shells. Average clutch size is 50 eggs. The sex of many species of crocodilians is determined by the nest temperature. Warm nests give rise to males, cool nests have females.

Birth

Just before birth, baby crocodiles call from inside their shells. This attracts the female to come and dig them out. Each has a caruncle on the top of its snout with which it breaks out of the shell. The mother will also roll the eggs gently between her teeth to help crack the shell. Nile crocodiles are about 11in long on hatching. They have strong jaws, but are still susceptible to predators. The female carries them from the water to the nest in a special pouch in her mouth. When in the river or lake they are guarded by mother in nursery areas. A shake of her body will send them into hiding below the water if a predatory bird appears.

Young

Saltwater crocodiles are protected by the mother for about 2½ months.

Fifteen percent will not reach their second month, but instead fall victim to the jaws of predators.

They grow to 17.5in in their first year and may live to be a hundred years old, if they can avoid the poacher's bullet.

The young Chinese alligator hatchling (right) has only survived because it has been bred in a zoo or on a crocodile farm. Persecution, pollution, and destruction of its habitat have contributed to the threat of extinction which now faces its wild relatives. So too has the increase in the skin trade, which has reduced population numbers.

Index

Photographic Credits:
Cover and pages 4, 20, 28 bottom, 29 and 30 top: Frank Lane Agency; pages 6, 24, 27 and 28 top: Planet Earth; pages 8, 16, 18 bottom, 20, 22, 25 and 31: Ardea; page 9, 10 middle and bottom, 12 bottom, 14, 18 top, 23 both, 29 top and 30 bottom: Bruce Coleman Ltd; pages 10 top and 15: Hutchison Library.

PRINTED IN BELGIUM BY
proost
INTERNATIONAL BOOK PRODUCTION